MW00377676

# Tears Of A Rose: Part 1

## A Collection of Poems, Free writes, And Spoken Word

## By: Akira Cavin

I dedicate this to my family. The Givens made me who I am today and for that, I thank all of you. For my mom, she is my rock.This is for my nieces and nephews, the reason why I still breathe. For my OG group, Poetic Asylum, the best artists known to man. We are truly #LyricallyInsane. This also goes out to all my family that has passed on to greater places. For grandma Dorothy, Uncle Danny, Auntie Betty, Aunt Bert, Uncle Lem, Pops,  and all others who have left us. You are truly missed. And last but not least, this one is for Yahree. Your legacy lives on forever. I love you big brother….

#LongLiveRee
#NoLabels

# Prologue

I have been writing poetry since I was 12 years old. When I wrote my first poem, it was two of my older brothers(Chaka and Yahree), that encouraged me to keep writing to get better. So I did. Every time I wrote a poem, they told me to save it. It would pay off one day. And I saved every single poem I could. Some were lost, but most of them I kept up with throughout the years. Now I have a huge collection of them. Each poem was written while I was in a certain emotional place and mindset. As I got older, my poems got better and they were able to resonate with those who understood not me, but the language poetry speaks.This particular collection of poetry is divided into two parts: elementary school and high school. So now, it's time to share the language of my life through the poems I write. I hope you like it. And I can promise you that the poems get better with time. You will see….

# Part One: The Elementary Years

Part one is mostly a collection of free writes and short poems that express my inner thoughts at a very young age. I was a curious child and I have always had questions or thoughts that I couldn't necessarily share with people. I took up writing at a very young age, but I was also bullied for a number of reasons, including not being able to speak up for myself. A small part of me had always wanted to ask questions and speak my mind and be confident in my words like I would see my siblings & cousins do. I envied how vocal they were, how strong they were, and I always wanted to be just like that, not realizing that I was my own person. I didn't know that I wasn't meant to fit in, I was supposed to stand out. But because I had never really done it before(except for in the academic area), I was afraid of someone not liking what I had to say. I wanted everyone to like me. I wanted everyone to be my friend so that things would be a fairy tale. But obviously life is not a fairy tale. So this first part of my book is a peek into how my mind wandered off whenever I needed it to be a place of serenity and openness...

# A Chains Mystery

Wearing a chain
can mean nothing,
something,
or everything
to a person.
We both wear a chain
that means everything to us.
I wear a diamond studded heart
necklace
that can be filled by anything
behind or in front of it.
My brother wears a silver dog tag.
The chain that I wear
represents my heart.
It can be shown so beautiful.
But on the inside,
It's just so empty and void
waiting to be filled.
The chain my brother wears
is still a mystery to the both of us.
Only he secretly knows.
And only he will secretly find out.
But even if it's no mystery to us,

it's still a chain's mystery…

# A True Master

The eye of a tiger
constantly watching and observing
whatever goes on.
The roar of a lion
being heard across the seven seas
making itself known.
The speed of a jaguar
running,
to catch its prey.
The pounce of a werewolf
tearing viciously into the flesh
of its deepest desires from its prey.
A true master
can kill a ferocious animal
in a split second
with his bare hands.
He can shed his powers
like the teardrop of a human.
That's the real power
of a true master.

# Pieces of A Puzzle

Life,
is like the pieces of a puzzle.
You never know
which piece goes where.
Or when there is a time & place
for everything.
If one piece doesn't fit another,
It's like a mistake being made
that can't be replaced
by just two simple words:
I'm sorry.
But, if it does fit,
then it represents letting go
and overcoming the mistake you've
made.
The moe you overcome a mistake,
the easier life gets.
As you grow closer to completing the
puzzle,
your life grows to an end.
Once the puzzle is complete,
it will start over.
And the puzzle of life continues

to start and end.
And even then,
time will start over.
Constantly repeating what it has
begun.
Like the pieces of a puzzle. Like the
puzzle of life.

# The Beauty of Nature

The gentle,
soft touch
of a human hand
caresses a delicate rose.
The texture of a rose
is like smooth red velvet.
That deep, dark red
hidden within the flower
as it perfectly funnels the stem
to protect the middle.
And as the petals gently touch your
cheek,
the little baby flowers start to bloom
with a tiny butterfly kiss
at the tip of your nose.
That is forever
and always will be
the beauty of nature.

# The Human Body

I wonder
how the human body works.
Adapting to its surroundings.
Working through thick or thin.
Studying.
Watching.
Observing what's around them.
Taking full advantage of what they have.
Killing and feasting
in order to stay alive.
Chopping wood and building houses
in order to survive.
What the eyes see
and the ears hear,
the mind believes.
One minute it's there,
then,

# Poof!

It's gone.
Vanished.
From dust we came
and to dust we shall return…

# Swagga Like Mines

I feel dominant over my possession.
Sometimes, I go crazy over confidence.
I sing, dance, and feel good about myself.
Haters look at me with jealous, envious
eyes
because they know they can't have what I
got.
They can't have a swagga like mines.

I keep my friends close
but my haters closer.
I love the way they try to push my buttons.
Some call me cocky.
But how could ya blame me?
Still, they don't have a swagga like mines.

They must love me
so they can hate me.
I love when they hate.
Because I know I'm a star.
For some reason, I've always noticed that

they don't have a swagga like
mines.*Inspiration: M.I.A.-Swagga Like Us*

# What Do You See In Me?

What do you see in me?
I'll tell you what I see.
I see somebody who's been hurt.
I see somebody who's been let down.
Disappointed many, many times.
But Mama sees a little bit of everything.
I just don't know what everything is.
All I want is a family.
A family that makes and keeps a promise.
A family that has my back through thick &
thin.
A family that will help me figure things out.
A family that will make me happy.
So I ask this question again.
What do you see in me?

# No One Knows

I am confused.
Everything was going to pass by too fast.
Sometimes people say they know my pain,
but they don't.
When I feel sad or depressed,
it's obvious that no one knows.


It seems as if I don't know
what's going on around me.
Because no one ever wants to tell me
what's happening around us,
I say something different.
It's obvious that no one knows.

Whenever I'm down,
there's no one to comfort me.
But that's just the way it is.
Some people can change their lives
because I know how they feel.
Still, it's obvious that no one knows.....

# Who I Am

I feel as if Africa runs through my blood.
Sometimes I am a singing machine.
So who do you expect me to be?
An African warrior princess is who I am.

Being natural is in my spirit.
When I am myself, it feels good.
What do you expect me to do?
An African warrior princess is who I am.

Sometimes I dance like the morning sun.
The cool air rushes through my hair.
How do you expect me to feel?
An African warrior princess is who I am.

When I feel the rhythm of my heart,
it feels as if the moon is my smile.
What do you expect me to be?
An African warrior princess is who I am.

# What I See?

What I see is pretty confusing to me.
Because no one else can see it.
No one else can see them.
I know that if they can't see them,
they can't feel them.
But I can.
Sometimes they are good and warm.
But other times they are cold and cruel..
I believe in the guardians.
Not the harmful.
Because I'm protected by the most
powerful.
He is my one and only Saviour.
But do you want to know what I see?
The guardian angel
God has sent for us…..

# This Season

It's the springtime.
So have fun with it.
Play sports or fly kites
before you miss the chance
you can barely get.

Have fun.
Ride bikes.
Enjoy the springtime air.
Absorb the freshness of flowers
or go to the town fair.

Let loose
your inner feelings
before you don't have them anymore.
Do whatever you can
to go through that open door.

Sometimes, it may not feel good.
But it only comes once a year.
So do what you want with it.
Because once it's gone,
You might want to shed a tear..

# The Raging, Changing, Beautiful Weather

Rain,
pours down from the heavens.
It can be as gentle
as a butterfly kiss
or as hard as a rushing waterfall.

Sunshine
glows upon all caring hearts.
It can be as warm
as a comforting, memory kept blanket
or as hot as a cooking oven.

The wind
blows & pushes everything, everywhere.
It can be as soothing
as a calm, deep breath
or as strong as a whirlwind.

This is the path
The journey
The only way
To love this beautiful weather of mine...

# You Are Forgiven

For all those times you left me hangin'
You Are Forgiven.

For all the moments you had me hurtin'
You Are Forgiven.

For all those days you betrayed me,
You Are Forgiven.

For all those no's you told me
But yes's you told everybody else,
You Are Forgiven.

For all the lies and deceit you made me
swallow
You have been…. Forgiven.

# From The Chain To The Lock

From the lock to the neck,
this chain keeps the black man's head
in a low, shameful position.
Yet he grows wiser as his head hangs.

From the lock to the wrists,
these chains keep the black man
from fighting back.
Yet he grows stronger as each day passes.

From the lock to the ankles,
these chains create the illusion that the
black man can only go so far before he's
back to where he started.
Yet he memorizes his way his way out.

And finally,
from the lock to the ground,
this chain keeps the black man in his place.
Yet he adapts to his surroundings…

# A Voice Never Spoken

Do you know what it's like
to be brilliant on the outside,
but so shameful on the inside.

That's because you pretend to be
what you know you aren't
because there was always something to
hide.

It's not like you have nothing to say
or nothing to think about.
Because all we do is think.

But have you ever considered the fact that
what happens in life
is not always about you?

Yeah.
I bet you haven't.
But you know you should.

Because I bet a thousand dollars
that this generation can do better

than what your generation could…

# Cancer

It spreads.
It fights.
It kills.
It dies.
It works.
It reproduces.
It affects the mind, body, and spirit.
It comes in many different ways.
It's the 1st leading cause of death in
America.

We have to be mindful
of what this disease can do.
It cuts your life in half,
just because it can.
It keeps you from your full potential
just because it wants to.

You can overcome it.
You can fight it.
You can beat it.
You can.. WIN.

# If You Only Knew

If you only knew
what I put up with
on a daily basis,
then we would see eye to eye.

If you only knew
what goes through my mind
as each day passes,
then, you would understand me.

If you only knew
what I went through
over the years of my life,
then, you would know the pain I feel.

If you only knew
what all those disappointments
has done to my heart,
then, you would be as mad as I am.

If you only knew
the physical pain I go through
on every single day of the week,

then, you would understand the condition
I'm in.

So the next time
you wanna cry about your crappy life,
think about mine first.

If you only knew…

# My Freedom

I want my freedom back
because it's something that I earned
and something I worked hard for.

I want my freedom back
because it's something I deserve
and I always broke a sweat for it.

Give me back my freedom
because my freedom
is not yours to take.

Give me back my freedom
because I completely refuse you
from taking what doesn't belong to you.

If you only knew
what my freedom means to me
only then you will leave me be.

# Do You?

Do you see what I see
with all this crime, violence,
and hatred around me?

Do you hear what I hear
with the negativity and police sirens
screeching in my ear?

Do you know what I know
about all this black on black crime
everywhere I go?

Do you feel what I feel
about how blacks can't find a safe place to
live?
Is this for real?

Can you see what I see
through all that hatred, crime, and violence
that is around me?

Can you know what I know
Besides all this crime

everywhere I go?

Can you feel what I feel
besides all this jealousy
that surrounds me?

Well guess what?


I see
a positive future
for me.

I hear
positive words
in my ears.

I know
That I can make it
Everywhere I go.

I feel
like I can be successful
in a world that is so very real.

# I Have

I have hatred
in my heart
because of what has been
done to me.

I have a nasty attitude
towards other people
because of the things
that won't let me be free.

I have negative energy
towards a lot of things
because of my eyes
not being able to see.

I have a closed mind
because of all the things
that limited me
from letting me be me.

Don't wind up like me.
Not being able to be me.
Go enjoy your life. Go be free…

# Me, Myself, & I

Me, myself, and I
is all I have
in this world.

Because whatever happens,
the second I touch it,
it shrivels and curls.

I don't have
anybody to lean on
or to talk to.

And whenever I'm in pain
no one is there
to bring me through.

Whenever I fall
nobody's lending a hand
to help me up.

But I am not
a little girl anymore.
I'm independent, strong, and tough.

Sometimes I feel like
I'm on my own
in this world.

But,
I will say this
I'm no ordinary girl.

# You Don't Deserve Me

You don't deserve me
because you didn't try
to break a sweat
to earn my trust.

You don't deserve me
because you treated me
like metal.
You left me there to rust.

You don't deserve me
because you don't know
and you didn't realize
the pain you caused me.

If you want to earn my love,
my trust, my respect,
then do your best and prove to me
that you can leave me be.

# Part Two: High School Years

My high school years were probably the most confusing and trying years in my life. A lot of pain I went through occurred in high school. But my escape was always writing. I would write whenever I had inspiration and I wouldn't be able to stop writing until I finished the poem. I always found peace after completing a poem. It was freeing. It felt like a small piece of the weight of my world was lifted one bit at a time with every word I wrote. And now that I am older and able to express that freedom differently, I want to be able to let young people

know that you are not alone in anything
that you do. Even if it feels like no one is
there for you, just remember that I am.
And I always will be.

Word of advice, please don't try to grow
up too fast. Enjoy your teenage years as
much as you can because if you don't,
you'll regret it.

# The Cold Eye

See a vision
that stops your heart.

View a mind
that tears words apart.

Decrypt a code
that takes a lifetime to create.

Look for a soul
that holds emotions to take.

Get a thought
that freezes you solid.

Intertwine a body
that can do what God did.

No one can imagine
the disappearance of the mind.

But what an amazing thing it is
to see with the cold eye.

# No Words

No words can describe
the pain I feel.

No words can explain
me seeing what was real.

You hurt me and you know it.
But you don't seem to care.

But if you do anyway
when I ask, will you be there?

To stand by my side,
to hold me, to love me?

Would you take off that blindfold
so that I can see?

In this series of questions
I have to ask one more.

Do you love me enough
to heal this sore?

I love you so much
but I feel like a lost bird.

But if you really love me,
You will tell me with no words.

# Why Not

Why not
show me the love
that I'm asking for?

Why not
give it to me
and I'll give you more?

Why not
show me your life
and I show you mine?

Why not
love each other & stay together
until the end of time?

# Until We Meet Again

We were once found together
As one meets the eye.

Through the rain and stormy weather
you caught me by surprise.

I saw it in your face
and felt it in my heart.

That you'd come and stay
with me as the other part.

Everything was going well
but it suddenly went downhill.

It couldn't just be simple
because I don't know how you feel.

What may happen between us
will always remain.

Because whether you like it or not
We are still one in the same.

We had problems so we split
and so did our soul within.

But my love is still there
until we meet again.

# The Perfect Struggle

We endlessly fought
and barely made it.

But we never gave up
because it was God who saved us.

We fought for our respect
and we stood up for our rights.

But loved ones are lost
In a vicious bite.

Barking dogs
Spraying water.

Children looking
for their father.

They beat us
with hard rubber.

But as a unit
we made the perfect struggle.

# Movin' On

As I speak my mind,
I'm letting you go.

I thought it would be nice
for me to let you know.

As you move on,
you are leaving my heart.

I don't want you to stay
but I don't want to be apart.

When I finally go on
and become myself again,

I just want you to know
that we can still be friends.

But when I am me again,
I hope it doesn't take long.

Because I'll do what I need to do
and I will finally be  movin' on.

# Who Is My King?

Who is my king?
He is a king of righteous kings
for whom I always praise.

Who is my king?
He is a king of merciful kings
from whom I worship when I hear his name.

Who is my king?
He is a king of shining kings
whose glory glistens night and day.

My king is a caring king
who is an extravagant inspiration.

My king is a helpful king
who guides me in the right direction.

I will always love and praise my king
and swim in his faithful, holy everlasting
pool

For as long as my king

sits upon his throne and rules!

# Unlimited Restriction

You have always been so open
to me doing whatever I want.

It seems as though you show me
everything you haven't taught.

But the minute I make my own choice,
everything is upside down.

You've shown my friends the many, many
ways
You make me look like a clown.

But I also wonder
do they feel the way I do?

Can they relate to me
Because they're in the same boat too?

I want to know so much
about the world's unknown depiction.

Because being your child

is nothing but unlimited restriction.

# Gone But Not Forgotten

There are memories
to share.

There are pains
to bear.

There is love
to hold.

And another life
to unfold.

There are faded joys
in the past.

And a path of anger
that lasts.

There are memories
we can keep.

So we no longer
have to weep.

If we hold on to
All the days and all the years,

We will no longer shed
another tear.

If you know what I know,
you know it was rotten.
You may be gone
but you are not forgotten.

# December 20th, 2010

Conversations on the cell phone
laughing and talking.

Loving the stories
then Sweetie came walking.

"Auntie! Auntie!
Mommy is crying!"

I walked into the bedroom
thinking she was lying.

"My son is dead! My son is dead!"
Cried my dear old mother.

R.I.P. Yahree Cavin.
We all needed to hug her.

Murdered by the police,
my brother was taken again.

And there he lay, dead and gone
on December 20th, 2010.

# My Dead Brother's Baby

He's just so plump and cute.
But he is a little spoiled.

He is just like his dad
Who always prevents turmoil.

He is sweet in every way
and he brightens up a room.

I'm glad he isn't trouble
and I pray he isn't doomed.

I will protect him with my heart
and befriend him with my soul.

I will dry his weary tears
and warm him when he's cold.

He is my dead brother's baby.
graven in his father's image.....

# The Perfect Black

Those piercing brown eyes
staring so innocently into the sky.

That plump little face
wondering what really lies.

The cutest little smile
that wants to say so much.

Those lovely baby fingers
that have the most gentle touch.

Who have thought
of the perfect devilish angel.

And his dad being
the perfect little stranger.

With the wish of returning
I know he can't come back.

But my brother has truly made
the perfect little black.

# A Better Place

Yes you have gone
and I know you can't come back.

It's a piece of me that is missing
one we all lack.

Sometimes I see you
and I feel your presence around me.

And I know that what happened to you
was not supposed to be.

We miss you and we love you
without a doubt in our hearts.

But somewhere in this world
we will never be apart.

So as life goes on,
you will be with us.

 But staying on this earth
will never be a must.

Even though you have left,
you will never go away.

Because I know you will be waiting
for me in a better place.

# A Rapper's Game

Isn't it funny
how one rhyme comes after another?

Sometimes it's about random things
but not often about lovers.

Newbies rap about their bling
and the way they wear their clothes.

But real rappers speak the truth
to a point where nobody knows.

It's amazing how they do what they do
and can earn so much.

And not be distracted
by love, envy, or lust.

I have seen some bogus rappers
and it's just a damn shame.

Because nobody knows like I do
about a true rapper's game.

# Together No More

When we first met
You quickly caught my eye.

And when we got together
your kindness was a surprise.

I loved the way you treated me.
I liked the way we talked.

My freshman year was fun
but I didn't like what I saw.

Our time together was good
and we really had no trouble.

But now we're parting ways
and you're leaving on the double.

I had to do what's best for me
and you're doing what's best for you.

You wanted to focus on your work
so you could walk out that door.

I'm with someone else now
Because we are together no more.

# Haterade

I'm tired of this fight.
I'm sick of this b.s.

I can't take it anymore.
It's just one big mess.

Over a boy though? Really?
You are seriously that petty?

I don't even care anymore
cuz my mind is already set.

So you mad at me
because I stopped you from being a hoe?

But since you jealous of what I got,
you should already know.

Seeing you suffer
Is just like drinking gatorade.

Cuz all you just did
was wash down some haterade.

# You Little Liar

You wanted to kiss me
and I told you no.

I wanted to be faithful
so that I wouldn't be low.

You knew I had a boyfriend
because you approved of him.

But I did know that
you weren't paying attention to them.

Cuz little did you know,
they would have told the truth.

But you kept pushing anyway
knowing that decision you would rue.

But my boyfriend is a great guy
and he will take me higher.

But when your choices blow up in your
face,

choose your fate you little liar.

# Start Over

What do I do
when I'm in need of care?

Between a rock and insanity
who will be there?

I can never be lost
but I was never found.

But will I get help
to stand up off the ground?

You loved me and you cared
and that I will never forget.

And I will always remember
how we first met.

Loving you is crazy
but I can handle it.

Because what you have showed me,
most people will never get.

The way you took care of me
Is like an alcoholic becoming sober.

Now that I have you
I have the strength to start over.

# Lovely Lady

Oh how pretty you are
and as smart as you can be!

Tiffany is your name
and I'm proud to call you mommy.

I love who you are
and everything that you do.

But it won't be long
Before I can reach you.

I miss you and I love you
and I care for you so much.

You have the best smile
and the gentlest touch.

Right now you are gone
but I'll be waiting when you come back.

So that we can hug and play
and share at least one more laugh.

I know you loved the day
that I became your baby.

But now I love the day
that you became my lovely lady.

# Cat & Mouse

Sometimes we connect
sometimes we don't.

Lust may have us both
but sometimes it won't.

We play & we flirt
even with our given history.

We may, but we may not
it will always be a mystery.

I want you, but not us
as I've told you so before.

My feelings are still there
But I'm walking out the door.

Me waiting waiting on you
is a wife waiting for her spouse.

We need to be serious
and stop playing cat & mouse.

# Silent Noise

Sometimes I feel like
I have no motives.

Because people see me like
just one big joke.

I have an opinion too.
I do have a mind.

But I can never say what I want
Because it "takes too much time."

Let me say what I wanna
so I don't feel shut out.

I'll do what I have to
so that I don't fill myself with doubt.

I may not be able to speak
but I do have a voice.

Because if I can't open my mind,
everyone will hear a silent noise.

# I Finally Got His Name

Waiting for so long
questioning and wondering.

Having doubts within myself
thoughts that are finally pondering.

After the torture of my dreams
and the beauty of my nightmares,

I have no one to talk to.
No one who really cares.

Sometimes I wonder
If my mind can fade away.

But if I over analyze again,
I can't see a brighter day.

Sgt. Mark M. Dolezal
is the man who played the game.

Best of luck inside his life
because I finally got his name.

# Unknown Familiar

I stand in the mirror
and I don't know who I see.

And then I ask myself
why did I do this to me?

I can look at myself
but not know who I am.

But if I don't start now
I won't get another chance.

I wanna be me again
and not someone else.

Because if I can't free my spirit,
then I can't live with myself.

My spirit is leaving my soul
is in the mind of a killer.

My evolution is almost complete
and I am becoming an unknown familiar.

# Secrets Untrusted

Trust is a kindness
something that has to be earned.

It comes with faithfulness
but never with bridges to burn.

I hate that I trusted like that
because now my secret is out.

No one will be safe
and that's without a doubt.

Whoever it was that told my life,
will seriously regret what they did.

And they will come to realize
that I am not a little kid.

Whoever did this to me
Will have a face that's busted.

And they will suffer at the utmost expense
because of my secrets untrusted.

# Trusted Betrayal

At first I thought you cared
and would put your children first.

But the things you've said & done
made me want to curse.

What happened to the love
you said you had for me?

But he climbed in my bed
and touched me when you couldn't see.

I feel lost and betrayed
and only you can make it better.

I can't hold it up any longer
so it's your time to keep it together.

I can't look at you the same
because you let me go through hell.

It doesn't seem like you cared
because you exposed my trusted betrayal.

# Scared Fearless

No one knows
the fear that eats at me.

Fear of loving
and not being able to see.

Someone, somewhere
is the most fearful person in the world.

But to scare my fear away
shows that I'm an extraordinary girl.

Death is lost, fear is gained
but life starts to fade inside.

To be scared of your own fears
means that there is nowhere to hide.

Holding on to what you've lost
is like frightening yourself senseless.

But to let go of what you think
is to believe that you're scared fearless.

# Life As In Death

Deep within in the mind
there is a treasure chest.

Tucked away is all your secrets
the ones you thought you laid to rest.

Love, life, and everything else
that was always mistaken.

Your best fears & worst dreams
Will forever be awakened.

Someone lost & something gained
is the relevance of life.

Nothing matters and never will
unless it causes strife.

Nothing gained, but always earned
Is better than the best.

Love, is like hate;
but it's life as in death.

To take a break from life is to make death seem irrelevant.

#Piensalo

# Source Of Sanity

Why does the world separate us so much?
We are put in these boxes with no air, no
space, and no.....sanity.
We are cut off from the future, yet isolated
from the past that just won't seem to be
gone but it just isn't..there.
But what about me?
What about how I feel?
If only someone could listen to the words
coming out of my mouth & the inner
thoughts of my heart and how about the
saying go "believe half of what you see and
most of what you hear?
Why can't my questions be answered?
Why can't my thoughts be processed?
Why can't I be pretty enough, or smart
enough, or strong enough, or cool enough,
or maybe even dumb enough?
But being at wit's end isn't where I'm
meant..to be.
It's not all bad but it's not all good either
because as I sit here with a gun to my
head, a knife to my wrist, a rope around my

neck, and the painkillers ready to launch, I
think to what has led me to this dark place
and how life would be once I am gone.
Will it still go on?
And that's the moment I remember what
the word VICTORY means to me.
And then, the gun is dropped.
The rope is loosened.
The painkillers down the drain & the knife is
neatly tucked back into the kitchen drawer
and I walk away from what I thought was
the solution to my problems.
And that is the moment I realized that the
dark place that once engulfed me, is no
longer my source of sanity.

# The Political Teenager

November 6th, 2012.
Working women & men wear their true
colors of their personal political party.
As the first presidential debates actually got
teenagers to tune into a world that has yet
to matter.
Well, almost anyway.
Anxious viewers vote as early as possible
to secure their savings into possibly elected
leaders.
Ah, but here's the good part.
They thought they had a voice.
But did you know that U.S. territories are
not represented in the Electoral College?
But after 57 election years and 44
presidents, it seems like we don't even
matter.
The early votes are casted out of
importance as election night votes were
elected into disposition of the unworthy.
If we don't choose the president, then who
does?

Because apparently the E.C. says jump
and we say how high.
Obama wanted equality & Romney wanted
selfishness.
As Obama shouted "Yes we can", Romney
murmured "Don't expect a big tax break."
Obama merely wanted to finish what he
started while Romney was secretly being
videotaped, which shows him disparaging
Americans who are tax-free at a dinner for
wealthy Republican donors.
He thought he had Obama one the fence of
the D during the 1st of 3 debates.
But that wasn't necessarily the case.
The 1st debate was attacked by Romney
but the script was flipped when Obama
talked into the issues that actually matter.
Then our country was split in two: 47% to
53%.
But guess who won?
My point exactly.
Case closed.

# I Need To Write

I need to write.
Write out the things I can't let go of.
All this anger needs to come out in some
way, shape, or form.
The way, shape, or form that is most
relative to this world.
My world.
The world that shoots, kills, and drives
people insane.
Insane to the point where the world has no
sanity.
No sanity to keep things in order.
In the order that lives up to impossible
standards.
Standards that are upheld by the way we
treat ourselves because we all too easily
forget what to do for our satisfaction.
The satisfaction that is accomplished in the
earth by the things of the earth which
doesn't benefit the imaginary reality on this
earth.

And this earth bears our sufferings &
shortcomings that will never disappear but
always remain unseen.
Unseen as to where it is beyond the point
of the naked eye but has yet to expose its
views under a microscope.
A microscope that zooms in & out of the
nebulas of this universe that houses
extraterrestrial beings that down at us from
millions of light years away, shaking their
heads and utter the words, "if Johnny had
never went to jail."
And as Johnny sits there in the
penitenti-area with unknown sights seen
about him, he sits & he writes.
Pen to paper, he pours out his emotions.
Johnny emptied out his little soul.
And he lets his hand glide across the paper
to let me know what gets bigger the more
you take away from it.
It's a hole by the way.
The way he left so many people whose
tempur-pedic mattress is now a five, six,
seven foot box, depending on how tall they
were.
They were all writers.

Writers of the mind, soul, and spirit.
Which is why I need to write.
Oh yeah, before I forget, Johnny was a
gang banger by the way.
He's a writer too…

# I Destroyed Myself

Sitting here just wondering
if my world is actually real.
Not knowing or caring about my own
thoughts or how someone else has picked
out my flaws.
I look at that screen & just feel my heart
sink to my knees as I yet again have cared
too much.
"I thought I could trust them…
I thought that they cared…
I thought that they loved me…"
And as my heart beats those words into my
chest, my lung collapses from hopeless
breaths that I wasted…on outworldly
people.
The people who were said to be my
"clique".
And as a social media post showed
sacrifices that they didn't know they were
making, my eyes saw everything.
My pupils dug deep into those words.
And at that instant, my heart swelled up
with pain, just like my infected gums.

Then, a sword snuck into my arms in the
place of my dad, who can't even look at me
in the face.
I guess I did do this to myself.
But now my fingertips are charred with
distress as the flag of my family burns its
life away.
I wish I could fix it.
I wish I could care.
But my big heart and noble love is what got
me into this bright darkness.
This realm of loneliness brings salty tears
to my face as I look in the mirror disgusted
by my own reflection & ask the question,
what have I done to me?
The necrosis of my searing body is no
longer attainable but is unbearable at the
mere thought of  destroying what is left of
myself.
My words no longer have purpose.
My hugs are no longer warm.
My mind no longer matters.
I guess that's what I get for being
everyone's snuggle buddy.

But hey, I guess I'll just have to cry a pond
of salty tears & talk to the moon until my
call gets a response.
I did destroy myself.
But I have to reap what I sow...
For now....

# Nothing But Silence

Not having anything to say
was always beyond me.

Saying too much
would make me a speech thief.

My opinion was too loud
and too strong for others.

My attitude was too sharp
for the bearing of my own mother.

I feel so out of place.
I'm so out of my element.

Sprewing educational beliefs
but with more than I ever meant.

So I've made my own choice
and I've decided on my mindset.

Since I've made too much noise
now there is nothing but silence.

# How Should I Say This?

How should I say the way that I feel?
Say what I feel to the airhead, the bougie
one, and the careless one?
One thing that only means my feelings
have been hurt.
Hurt by the words & pictures that were said
and shown to me.
And me not knowing how to hide it.
To hide and despise the fact that they really
don't care.
I feel like an idiot for letting them do this to
me.
How many times should I go through this?
How many times should I cry?
How many times should I allow my
sensitive interior collapse to nothing?
I still haven't figured that out yet.
I guess I'm just the girl who's just there.
I'm the girl nobody likes.
I'm the girl who they don't care about.
I'm just the alternate.
Now I understand how an understudy feels.
But these feelings should not last for long.

Just until I figure out how to say this…..

# That Childhood Place

Have you ever wondered
what it would be like
to have all your dreams come true?
Maybe if it's the pink pony, the hot wheelz
space rocket, or wish to have a million and
one dollars inside your tiny little piggy bank
locked up in that special box in the remote
corner of your closet.
But, what if you opened that intricate lock
with a key to that box that will always be
the little kid with a dream.
What will happen then?
That's when all of your untimely tires and
deepest desires are splashed into the
daylight of reality that only accepts the
modern world of PR firms & laws of
metaphysics & Family Guy's dirty jokes.
But what if these dreams....come true?
What if you did own the prettiest palace in
all the land or the blind stealth of a secret
ninja or the golden guns of 007?
Or what about the dream to be the most
famous singer in all the world or the wish to

be the best at air guitar or the most epic
rock & roll star throughout the "almost"
United Empire of Earth?
What about that hope?
What about that dream?
What about that drive….to be the best?
When we were 6, the answers were valid.
They were valid when our challenges as
children were just learning how to tie our
shoes.
They weren't important.
But now that we're all grown up, the people
of this society expect a real answer.
Well, why should they?
Oh, I know why.
But do you?

# One More Too Many

Why is it
That my loved ones have to suffer?

They seem as if they are no longer good
like they're just old mufflers.

What do I do?
What should I say?

How can I heal them
to make their pain go away?

Auntie Betty was first
then Uncle Vino was next.

Then there goes Uncle Danny
and laid Yahree to rest.

Lastly is Aunt Bert
Whose trail is left too trendy.

But I refuse to let go of Grandma Dorothy
because she is one more too many.

# The Room

White robes are spotted with civilian
clothing.
And my grandma was among the white
robes.
White robes disguised with familiar faces
as the sun's grazing bled through the
windows of… the room.
A room where I… am dressed in civilian
clothing.
But my family wore otherwise.
I sit there and I talk to my grandma.
Reminiscing and missing the old memories
of our glory days.
Glory days that fade away with the rising
daze that numbs my mind into the wishing
ways of the naive little girl who clings to her
grandmother for help.
She grows older.
Old enough to know what the word "sick"
really, really means as the older generation
chugs closer to their end of days.
I talked to her.
We laughed.

I fed her.
We hugged.
I missed her.
As the clock on the wall hit the stroke of twelve, a civilian tapped me on the shoulder and asked, "Who are you talking to?"
I replied, "My grandma."
Then it hit me.
He said, "How are you talking to your grandma if no one is right there?"
And that's when I realized that I was the only civilian who could see the people in the white robes.
Only then did I notice that those who wore the white robes were all deceased.
My grandma had simply came from heaven to visit me.
She saw that I needed her.
And right before I uttered the words "Grandma, I love you!" I was awakened by my re-energized body.
I never got the closure.
I didn't get the chance to say I love you as she rested on her deathbed.
I hope I get to see her again.

I hope she knows I love her.
And I hope that when we meet again, we
will be together in…
The Room.

# Unnaturally Perfect

Living in a world that's hard to please
doesn't make my confidence better.
Imitating & Emulating what others do and
say shouldn't be a processed pattern of
performance.
Cutting pieces to copy cat & correct what
I've already done.
What we've already done.
You see it's not enough to do what we did
but you try to speak and cover it up to avoid
confrontation.
Confrontations concluding conversations
that burst into laughter that mockingly
leaves in the ground what someone
thought they could say.'
But I just sit here, shaking my head &
returning the old song "Another One Bites
The Dust."
Laying down my mind, mesmerizing
meteors making movements towards that
spinning spherical circle, or ball (I should
say) and just wondering when will the
original reality hit.

Writing pen to organized, stained paper
makes me need to continue this poem.
This rhetoric repeating rhymes to douze in
information unnecessary & un-repetitive to
the actual tips of my elongated fingers.
But still this world has yet to learn what it
really means to be actual.
Facing the actual fact that nobody loves
perfection.
And yet we all still call out to our
conscience & trying to make it bleed
internally the thing we all desire.
But who's to say that we are all unnaturally
perfect?
Any takers?

# My Beloved Father

From the moment you held me
in your loving arms,
I knew that you loved me
and I would never be harmed.
From my first pair of K-Swiss
to my first father-daughter date,
it was you who was with me
so that I would never escape.
It was you who loved me.
It was you who cared.
It was you who cared.
It was you who promised
to always be there.
True to your word
you have become the light of my day.
So it's now, I say to you
Happy Father's Day!

# Letter To My Love

Since we have met
we were the closest of friends.
We have grown and we have learned &
thought that the happiness would never
end.
Junior year we started what seemed to be
the perfect match.
But all of our struggles were way too far
from that.
I loved you like I've never loved before.
But it seems like our love & need to be free
was just another locked door.
So yes he's back and please don't hate me
for wanting to try again.
But I want you to know that my love for you
will never end.
For now we might have to go our separate
ways.
But I promise that will never fade.
One day it will work, our love will come to
pass.
Just like those old folks say
"An old flame will never last."

I love you…

# I Don't Remember

A few of them are gone already with a legacy left behind.
Faded joys and hurtful times that only a memory cana capture.
Auntie Betty was the 1st one to go.
She was the everlasting but no longer living glue that our family held on to.
For years she would light up a room with her eyes, tell a story with her smile, and every single one of the little ones were blessed with a sweet forehead kiss and a warm embrace.
And yet, I can't even remember what her favorite color is.
But cancer knows.
It slowly ate away her eyes, withered away her smile, and took away that one last kiss goodbye.
And she didn't even have a funeral.
Her selfish daughter allowed her to suffer and die slowly but then cremated her body so that we couldn't even honor her memory.

Uncle Vino was next.

He physically distant but spiritually close.

Well, that would give the great Richard Pryor a run for his money.

He was always the uncle who nobody will ever forget as long as they heard him tell a joke.

But now I can't even remember who his favorite comedian is.

And as a brain leakage got to him, distance got to us.

In the hospital for days, he hung on for dear life as his spirit struggled to enter and exit his body.

Finally, he let go.

And since his body was in Iowa and mine was in Chicago, there was a funeral there and a memorial service here.

After that, it was Uncle Danny.

This was a man who could get all the ladies and take them all to the same meet & greet without conflict.

But years of drinking finally caught up with him.

Reading his check info told us that he had lung cancer and cirrhosis of the liver.

The doctor gave him a timestamp of a few
months  while he literally withered away to
nothing.
And while he slowly started forgetting what
his favorite juice was.
But my dream foretold when he would die
as I woke up out of it only ten minutes
before he did.
Funeral services were held with an open
casket to a stranger because he no longer
looked the same.
But I just can't seem to remember…..

# In His Likeness

I bet no one has ever stopped to realize
where their soul came from.
But it's a very simple logic, you see.
There is a higher being as to which we all
belong.
 But I guess no one really cares about that
part.
Maybe it's because he doesn't physically
walk among us.
And even though his state of mere
existence is so very far beyond the human
mind & the human...ego.
I know that God is real.
I know that He is my provider.
And though He is not physically with us, our
mental capacity is that of daphnia to the
great Albert Einstein.
But, ah.
Here's the trick.
See now people seem to believe that since
the Lord Almighty sent his only son to
possess the earthly flesh born to deprive
mankind of sins that we have grievously

have committed against the light of the
world, which is free of the hell-bound death
we call sin, which is on our level.
And yet, he isn't.
We are a small speck of sand amongst all
the beaches of the world which seems to
have no care for the speck right next to it.
But still, God loves us through it all.
We are like a nanosecond around the clock
which is still waiting for a day of eternity.
And still we are loved. Still we are cared
for. Still we are provided for. We Still are
healed.
After all, weren't we made in his likeness?
But hey,
who listens to an 18 year old girl who is
made in God's image(according to her
calculations) and was, & is being taken
care of by
The. Holy. Trinity.
So to prove the atheist's disbelief, yes I am
made in his likeness.

# To Music

It all started way back when in 2010, when my brothers talked about and dedicated their life to you.
They said, "To music, may it be the one thing that keeps my little sister happy."
That's when I began to fall in love.
In love with the idea of being in love with the one thing that could save my life forever and truly let their hearts speak to mine as if to say, "Man, music sure did make you happy."
Slowly and gently we became mutual friends as if we had anything better to do with life besides satisfy ourselves.
Your love spoke before my feelings could immerse themselves into the deep red personification of courage and beauty.
But even then, your melodic voice, your sensitive touch, and that one glorious kiss you always leave lingering on my lips as I start to adore you.
I treasure you.

I make you my escape plan from life,
liberty, and the pursuit of perfection so
many dead souls grievously try to reach
with sophisticated hand signals, deafening
heavy metal, and the injections that create
our face comes to shackles around my
ankles.
But you, my music, has saved me.
Me and my weirdness, me and my
sovereignty, me and my family, and me and
my shambles.
The shambles, leaks, holes, pockets, and
cracks that only you, music, can remove.
And when that moment comes that my
virgin ears will be penetrated with a whole
new sound and a whole new way that my
music can handle, it will be extraordinary.
But I still need your dedication, music.
I need you to be there for me, music.
I need to know that you, my music, will be
the only one to love me like one else can.
So, here it is.
To music, my poem for you.

# Love Hates Us

Tears are shed
crying of pain, loss, and sacrifice that goes
unworthy.
It hurts.
I can't give him up in my mind and in my
heart because he came too close to being
one with us.
Even the mere thought of losing him to a
love that I can't have beats my head into a
comatose state of unhappiness as my
smile is removed from my face.
My eyes no longer gleam.
My heart no longer beats.
My mind is snatched out of the cloud of
fantasy and placed back in between a rock
and a hard place.
"Baby please don't leave me! You can't
leave me! Please baby don't do this to me!"
Those words climb out of his soul to the
tips of his fingers to reply to what was the
most painful message I have ever sent in
my life.
It hurts.

It hurts so much.
This pain that is ripping at my veins &
eating at my chest begins to sicken me.
My stomach hurts.
My head is spinning. My eyes are burning.
My chest is collapsing.
I can't do this anymore.
But even now, as he is no longer welcome
and permanently unapproved, he still
doesn't get it.
He gave up on us.
So I had to give up on him.
I may not ever stop hurting, but until then,
this poem is done crying.

# What Has He Done To Me?

Missing him,
wanting him every second of every minute
of every hour as each day passes.
Is this what it feels like?
My mind sits back dazed at the fact that
love actually happened.
Perpetuating lovely ideas under false
pretenses of the glorious 4 letter word that
did not meet his part until the date 12-21-12
started to reign forever.
Stuck between a love and a hard place, my
shattered heart takes a leap of
faith(towards a love, of course) only to find
the intertwined musical spirit of the love I've
always wanted.
I dream of him and I sit in sleep to lay in
wonders of what our life would be like.
Will it treat us fairly?
Will our love, the only thing that even death
won't break, love us back?
I'm terrified of sooner separation but joyous
of future endeavors as I tirelessly work my

heart and soul to love him the way he has loved me.

"I missed you baby," is followed by a warm hug and a soft sensual kiss with a closeness wanted all the time and needed everyday, sprinkled with laughter & my favorite "I love you" cherry on top.

Damn man, what has he done to me?

And I wonder if he tells the moon to relay the message to me that he is there and he wants me.

I crave him inside my soul to be one with my body & spirit only in hopes that he will stay.

And even though I have to let him go, what loves me the way I love him is his love itself.

And that will always come back to me, with him standing right next to it, just to tell me that he loves me one more time.

And even then, he will still be mine 12-21-12 forever…

# Hatred Of No Name

Red eyes
painful words
tears shed with discomfort and disgrace as
he begins to hate me.
But now, I no longer require his love.
I no longer need his mercy.
I am no longer his beloved daughter.
Those shards of hatred hurt me to the
inside of the core of my soul as a heart
attack comes into play.
So many years of abuse has used me and
my intellectual being that does nothing but
hide.
It only hides the rides of negative surprises
inside as it is tucked away under guard,
lock, and key while I have to draw a
s.m.i.l.e. onto my face.
He disowned me.
He hates me.
I hear these terrible words again and again
as my guilt eats my flesh like a necrotic,
incurable disease.
But you know what,

I DON'T CARE ANYMORE!
I've found a doctor called ignorance that
prescribed an extra large dosage of
nonchalant behavior towards an empty
pain.
I now pronounce you dead in my presence,
nonexistent in my past, and below nothing
in my future.
You wanna know hate?
Well how's that for hate you bastard.

# Hey! You There!

Yes you! The one who made it to the end of this book! My name is Akira and I want to personally thank you from the bottom of my heart for taking time out of your life to read something so special to me. I appreciate all the support that you have shown and I want to show my gratitude to you. But I need your help.

Go through the book one more time and make a list. The list should consist of your top 20-25 poems from this book and also any questions you may have. What I will need you to do is send me an email with your list & questions.Then, I will re-release this book with the backstories to each poem you have selected AND the answers to all of your questions.

You can simply shoot me an email at AkiraKPoetry@gmail.com or message me on social media on my Twitter & Instagram: @AkiraK_ThePoet.

Thank you so much again and I can't wait to give you all the part 2 to this book! Stay tuned!

Made in the USA
Coppell, TX
16 August 2021

60587825R00069